Project Nemesis

and Other Mysteries

Compiled by Tony Bradman

Stories by
Tony Bradman, Helen Dunmore
and Philippa Pearce

Illustrated by Adrian Barclay,
Sholto Walker, Rosamund Fowler
and David Frankland

Contents

Project
Nemesis

Written by Tony Bradman

Illustrated by Adrian Barclay

'And another thing, Dean,' said Dad, tapping the steering wheel as he glowered through the windscreen. The car in front hadn't budged for the last ten minutes. 'You were very late going to sleep last night. It was past twelve when I came in and I'm pretty sure I heard your computer.'

'You couldn't have, Dad,' said Dean hurriedly. He had switched it off and dived under his duvet the instant he'd heard Dad's feet on the stairs. 'I was in bed *long* before ten o'clock. Honest, I swear.'

Dad sighed and turned to face him. Dean realised they had reached the stage of his father's lectures when Dad would start talking in his 'let's-be-grown-up-about-this' tone of voice. Now it was Dean's turn to glower through the windscreen and silently pray for the traffic to un-jam.

'Look, Dean,' said Dad. 'We both know you were playing one of those dreadful games. You never seem to do anything else at the moment. Don't you get tired of blowing people apart and splattering brains everywhere?'

'Computer games aren't all like that, Dad,' said Dean, offended. Why was it adults always thought the worst of the stuff kids enjoyed?

'I don't just play shoot-'em-ups, anyway. They're OK but I like strategy games best. *Sim City, World Domination, Megabyte War …* '

'That's all very well,' said Dad. 'But your mother and I just wish you'd spend a bit more time doing your homework, and a bit less playing computer games. They can't possibly be doing you any good, can they?'

Dean fumed inside. What did Dad know about it? Dad had never actually played a computer game in his life, so he had no idea how difficult some of them could be. They were much more demanding than most homework. You needed a whole range of skills to play them.

Not that there was any point telling Dad that. He simply wouldn't believe it. As far as Dad was concerned, they were *games*, and games meant *fun*, which you obviously weren't supposed to have. Ever.

'I'll try, Dad,' said Dean, arranging his face in that especially sincere expression he reserved for use during a Dad lecture. Total surrender was usually the only means of bringing the agony to an end.

'I'm glad to hear it,' said Dad, and Dean relaxed, sensing that this morning's Bore-A-Thon was probably over. It hadn't really been that bad, either, he thought. About four point five on the Dad Drone-O-Meter.

Dean had been expecting a nine, at least. Dad had been very grumpy all week. There seemed to be some sort of crisis at the office and Dad had been getting home later and later every night. This morning Dean had heard him telling Mum he would have to work through the weekend.

Mum had not been pleased. And Mum could be a holy terror when she was cross. Dean was relieved he'd be spending *his* weekend sleeping over at his best friend's place. He was going straight to Jamie's house with him immediately after school finished.

'I think the traffic's about to move, Dad,' said Dean, peering up the road over the stationary cars. The lights had changed from red to green.

'Is it?' muttered Dad, his eyes snapping to the car in front. Dean noticed an edge of desperation in his voice. 'You're right, thank goodness. I should have been at the office ages ago. Put the radio on, will you?'

Dean reached forward and pressed the FM switch.

' ... *continued major traffic jams throughout the Greater Metropolitan area this Friday a.m.,*' an announcer was saying. '*Reports are also coming in of a series of bizarre incidents involving the emergency services ...*'

'Oh no!' groaned Dad. Dean glanced at his father. Dad was listening to the radio as if his life depended on it. His whole attention was focused on the announcer's words. Dean was puzzled. Why should Dad be so worried by a news story about police cars and fire ambulances turning up at the city's TV studios for no apparent reason? Dean shrugged.

He would never understand grown-ups.

'You can let me out if you like, Dad,' he said. 'It's only ten minutes' walk from here and the lights have changed again.'

Dad's shoulders slumped.

'You don't want me to be late for school, do you?'

'Certainly not,' said Dad, pulling sharply to a halt at the kerb. There was an angry honk from the car behind. Dean opened the door and heard sirens wailing in the distance.

'Bye, son,' said Dad as Dean got out. Dean had hardly shut the door before Dad pulled back into the line of cars. He was still stuck in the same place when Dean turned the corner.

'Are you sure we can get away with this, Jamie?' whispered Dean. He shifted uncomfortably on the swivel chair and glanced at his friend. It was late that Friday evening and the two boys were sitting side by side at Jamie's desk. 'I mean, my dad will kill me if he finds out.'

'You worry too much,' said Jamie, his eyes focused on the glowing computer screen in front of them. 'He's not going to find out. We'll just log on, have a look around, then vanish like a pair of cyber-ghosts. OK?'

No, it wasn't OK, Dean thought uneasily but he didn't say anything. He knew there was simply no stopping his friend once he'd picked up the scent of a new site he could hack into.

Jamie thought he was the High Priest of Teen Hackers, a super-duper Net snooper from way back.

Things had been fine until Dean had let slip he knew the password Dad used to access his office computer. Dad was always forgetting it so he kept it written on the pad by the phone. Jamie's ears had pricked up and it hadn't taken him long to extract the password from Dean.

From that moment on Jamie just couldn't wait for his mum and dad to go to bed. He hadn't even wanted to sneak down and watch the late, late horror movie on cable. He'd had one activity on his mind, and one alone. And that was hacking into Dean's dad's office computer.

Dean had done a little light hacking with Jamie before and their usual targets were relatively risk-free. They *had* penetrated the school records database a couple of times but the most exciting piece of information they'd uncovered there was the Head's middle name.

Dean's dad, however, worked for an organisation that was rather more important and potentially more dangerous for hackers – the government.

'Hey, we're in!' said Jamie triumphantly. Dean's heart sank. A list of government departments was swiftly scrolling up the screen.

'What exactly does your dad do?' asked Jamie, his fingers still clicking on keys.

'How should I know?' said Dean.

'You're a great help, aren't you?' said Jamie. 'Right, I think we'll try … *this* one,' he said, and clicked firmly on a large, shield-shaped icon with a lightning flash and the words *Central Security* emblazoned on it.

Password and coding questions filled the screen one after the other. Jamie started trying to field them but Dean could see his friend was struggling. Dean felt his reluctance giving way to curiosity and the urge to face the challenge this distant computer was throwing at them.

It was no contest for them together. Twenty minutes later, Dean and Jamie were browsing through some files with impressive titles. *Buildings Security, Personnel, Links to Intelligence Agencies.* That one was even marked *Top Secret* … Dean started to feel uncomfortable again.

'Wow!' said Jamie. 'That is *so* cool!' A small, simple window had appeared. Inside it was a single word – *Nemesis* – and the image of a grinning, silver and black death's head.

Nemesis

'I just *have* to see what it is,' said Jamie, and clicked on the icon before Dean could stop him.

'Er … Jamie,' he said. 'I have a bad feeling about this.'

'Relax,' said Jamie, his fingers flashing. 'We're on a roll now, old buddy. Besides, what could possibly happen? They'll never find us.'

Suddenly the window in the screen vanished and a new one appeared. Inside it were a lot more words. *'Warning! System accessed by unauthorised terminal. Online search initiated … proceeding …'*

'Oh no,' muttered Dean, watching in horror as the word '*proceeding*' blinked in the corner of the window. 'Do something, Jamie!'

'I don't have to, Dean,' said Jamie, leaning back smugly. 'I've seen this kind of stuff before. It's like the *X-Files* website. You log on and a warning comes up saying the FBI is on its way to arrest you. It's a joke.'

'I'm not laughing,' said Dean. 'And I'd be a lot happier if we logged off this particular site … *right now*. I don't know about you but I have plans for my life, and they don't include spending a large chunk of it in prison.'

'OK, OK,' said Jamie with a sigh. 'If you're going to be a wimp.'

Jamie clicked on the window – but couldn't get it to close. He clicked again, and again, his brow furrowed, and still nothing happened.

Then the word '*proceeding*' was replaced by … '*TRACED*'.

'Just turn it off, Jamie,' said Dean, his voice rising in panic.

Jamie didn't have to be told twice. He reached past Dean and jabbed the off switch. The *Nemesis* window folded in on itself and the screen went dark.

Both boys let out a sigh and turned to look at each other.

'I'll bet it was a trick to put hackers off,' said Jamie with a nervous laugh.

Dean knew he was trying to convince himself as much as anyone.

'You're probably right,' said Dean, and Jamie smiled.

But later, as Dean lay stiffly in his sleeping bag on Jamie's bedroom floor, he couldn't get a particular image out of his mind. And that silver and black death's head pursued him relentlessly through his dreams …

Dean was in a locked room, cowering in the corner, and somebody – or *something* – was pounding at the door, trying to smash through it and get him. Then he realised he was dreaming and opened his eyes.

But the pounding continued.

Somebody *was* hammering at the front door of the house, and there were plenty of other noises too – loud voices, running feet, a whooshing, beating sound that seemed to be coming from above the roof.

'Wow, a *chopper*,' shouted Jamie. Dean sat up and saw his friend kneeling on the bed. He was looking out of the window. '*A-mazing*.'

'What's going on?' Dean yelled.

'No idea, pal,' Jamie shouted happily. 'But I have a feeling we might well be in a little trouble. I *don't* believe it. I've just seen a guy with a *gun* out there! Hey, it's a whole SWAT team, and they're all over the garden!'

Dean groaned and burrowed deep into his sleeping bag.

But there was no escape. He heard Jamie's dad stomp down and open the front door, followed by Jamie's mum. There was a shouted conversation in the hall with somebody outside. It sounded quite heated.

At last, several pairs of feet thumped up the stairs and the bedroom door was opened. Jamie's dad put his head round and spoke.

'You two had better come downstairs,' he said grimly.

Dean caught a glimpse of helmets behind him on the landing. Each one bore a distinctive symbol – a shield containing a lightning flash and the letters *CS* …

A few moments later, Dean and Jamie were sitting on the sofa in the front room. Jamie's dad was sitting in one armchair and his mum in another. Dean could tell that both of them were pretty angry.

There wasn't much they could do though. An armed SWAT team member was standing by the door. Another armed man with three stripes on his dark-uniformed arm was speaking quietly into a radio headset.

'Central from Alpha Squad,' he said. 'Location secured, over.' Then he turned to Jamie's mum and dad. 'Someone will be arriving soon who will be able to answer your questions. If you could remain patient …'

'Cool,' whispered Jamie, nudging Dean. 'It's just like the scene in *Final Strike III* when the rogue SWAT team wipe out that family …' Jamie noticed his dad glaring at him. 'Er … sorry, Dad,' he said, and shut up.

'This is outrageous,' said Jamie's mum. 'How dare you barge into my house with some wild story about national security. I won't …'

She didn't get a chance to finish.

Just then, two more people entered the room. Dean glanced up and swallowed hard. One was a tired-looking man with staring eyes. He was carrying a shiny, aluminium briefcase.

The other was Dean's dad.

'Thank you, Sergeant,' Dad said to the man with the headset. 'I'll take over from here. You and your men can get back to base.'

The sergeant saluted and slipped out with his fellow SWAT team member. Once the door was closed behind them, Jamie's mum and dad leaped to their feet and started shouting at Dean's dad. Then Jamie's dad suddenly stopped and peered more closely at the man in front of him.

'Hang on,' he said suspiciously. 'But you're Dean's dad, aren't you? I think we've met before, haven't we? At the school open evening? Don't tell me, this is all a set-up for one of those funny TV programmes, isn't it?' He grinned at his wife. 'I'll bet there's a hidden camera somewhere.'

'I'm afraid there isn't,' said Dean's dad. 'What's happening is very real. Now, if you'll just sit down, I'll try and explain everything to you as quickly as I can. Then I have something to ask these two.'

'It's OK, Dad,' said Dean gloomily. 'I confess. Jamie and me hacked into your office computer. But we could never have done it if I hadn't supplied the password. It's all my fault, really. I'm sorry.'

'I'm glad to hear it,' said Dad with a wry smile. 'But I already knew you were the culprits, actually, and I had another question in mind. How would you boys like to *help* us – the government, that is?'

For a second Dean wondered if he was still dreaming after all...

'It sounds like an absolute *nightmare*,' Jamie's mum was saying, taking a mug of tea and a biscuit from the tray Jamie's dad had just brought in. 'Although I'm not quite sure I understand everything you've told us.'

'Come on, Mum,' said Jamie, rolling his eyes at Dean. 'It's dead simple. The government developed some fancy new software designed to unite all official computers into one big system. They installed it last month, there was a bug in it, and it's gone wrong. Like HAL in *2001*, or the big computer in *The Terminator* and *Terminator 2*.'

'That's right,' said Dean's dad. 'In fact, the system is responding in an extreme way, almost as if it's being threatened. When a traffic control video camera records someone going through an amber light, the system picks it up and instantly changes every light in the city to red.'

'Oh, I *see*,' said Jamie's mum. 'Now we know why the traffic was so awful everywhere this morning. And you say things are getting worse?'

Dean listened, fascinated. Part of the system monitored TV broadcasts, and was ordering police and ambulances to the studios every time someone seemed to be hurt in films or cartoons. Another part had sent the Defence Secretary to a bunker to protect him three days ago, then locked him in.

Yet another had sent out a full SWAT team when Dean and Jamie's hacking was traced, although in fact they'd been lucky. The system had ordered a tactical air strike when some adult hackers had been detected. Only a frantic, last-minute phone call to the airbase had saved them.

Dad said he'd been given the task of coordinating the attempt to deal with the crisis. But like most of the senior people working for the government, he knew nothing about computers. So they had called on some experts, a team led by the man who had come with Dad.

His name was Professor Lloyd and he had been working round the clock. No wonder he seemed exhausted.

Dad was looking pretty tired too, thought Dean.

'OK, I think we're clear on all that now,' said Jamie's dad. 'But what I still don't understand is how Jamie and Dean can help you.'

'Over to you, Professor,' said Dad. 'That's *your* department.'

'Well, it's quite straightforward really, if a little embarrassing,' said the computer expert, and smiled nervously. 'As soon as the first problems occurred we installed a radical clean-up programme – *Project Nemesis*. But the system closed it down and no one has been able to get to it since.'

Dean and Jamie looked at each other.

'We did,' they said in unison.

'Exactly!' said Professor Lloyd, excited. 'We can still monitor some of what's happening in the system, so we knew you'd hacked in. We checked your response times and they're incredible! Better than any of the … *adults* in my team. We believe you're the only people who can reactivate *Nemesis* and debug the system before there's a major catastrophe.'

'But we only saw the icon,' said Dean. 'We didn't have time to get into the programme before this other window flashed up and cut us off.'

'Ah, that was probably because the terminal you were working with wasn't powerful enough,' said Professor Lloyd. 'We're certain that if you had something a little more beefy …' he said, opening the aluminium briefcase and displaying its contents, '… you'd get a lot further.'

'Whoa!' said Jamie, awestruck. 'That's a top-of-the-range THX 1138!'

'You *do* know your computers, don't you?' said Professor Lloyd, impressed. 'So, do you two think you can handle this little baby? We can just plug it straight in and away you go.'

'*Can* we?' said Jamie. 'Watch us! It'll be a doddle, won't it, Dean?'

'Yeah, I suppose so,' said Dean. Then he paused and looked at his father. 'But I have the feeling something is missing here, Dad. What happened to all that stuff about how bad playing computer games is for me? Or does this prove they can do kids good as well?'

'OK, you win,' said Dad. 'I agree, they've obviously done *something* to your fevered brain and I'm grudgingly prepared to admit the effect might even be good. I'm certainly hoping it will come in useful as far as saving the world is concerned. And I don't mean to hurry you, but …'

'One last question, Dad,' said Dean, smiling. 'Seeing as Jamie and me *are* about to save the world, is there any chance we might be in line for some kind of … well, reward? You know, something like large amounts of money, new computers, hundreds of new computer games?'

'How about total immunity from criminal prosecution for illegal hacking?' said Dad, smiling back. 'And if you're really lucky, I might even provide some support when you tell your mother what you've been up to. Somehow I don't think she's going to be too happy with you.'

'Er ... OK, Dad,' said Dean hurriedly. 'It's a deal. Right, Jamie. Time we got upstairs and started kicking some computer butt. Coming, Dad? You never know, if you pay attention, you might even learn something.'

'Oh, I doubt that, Dean,' said Dad with a smile. 'I doubt that very much.'

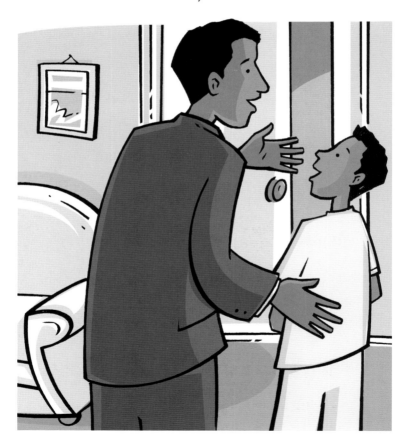

Aliens Don't Eat Bacon Sandwiches

Written by Helen Dunmore

Illustrated by Sholto Walker

My brother Dan has been making his own bacon sandwiches since he was ten years old. It's not that he likes cooking that much – it's just that no one else knows how to make the perfect bacon sandwich.

He'd get everything ready by the cooker first. Bacon, bread, tomatoes, ketchup, sharp knife. The bacon had to be fried fast, so it was crisp but not dried up. He'd lay it on one slice of soft white bread, smear it with ketchup, cover it with tomato slices, and then clap a matching white slice on top. Then he'd bite into it while the bacon was hot and the fat was soaking into the bread.

Dad used to say that Dan would go to Mars and back if he thought there'd be a bacon sandwich at the end of it. Don't forget this. The bacon sandwich is important.

Then there was the portable telephone. We should never have bought it, Mum said. I mean, I like talking to my friends on the phone, but Dan was something else. He was never off it. When he came in from school he'd pick up the phone right away and call someone he'd only been talking to half an hour before. And they'd talk and talk and talk. Sometimes Mum would come in and stand there tapping her watch or mouthing 'phone bill!' at him, but it never seemed to make much difference. Dan was a phone addict.

I was cleaning my bike in the garden one day, and Mum and her friend Susie were talking about telephones and big bills and teenage kids. Susie said, 'It's all right as long as you realise that teenagers aren't people at all really. They're aliens from outer space. That's why they spend all their time on the phone. They have to keep in contact with other aliens who come from the same planet.'

I didn't take much notice of what Susie said at the time, but it came back to me later. Mum leaned back in her deckchair and laughed. She'd been out on a location all day, taking photographs: Mum's a photographer. She was working on a feature about corn circles. I expect you've seen pictures of them. Perfect circles in wheat, much too perfect to have been made by wind or rain. There were more of them than ever that year, and nobody knew how they came.

At first the newspapers said it was a hoax. Reporters and photographers used to sit up and keep watch all night by cornfields, to catch the hoaxers. But they never did. Somehow they'd get sleepy and doze off and then when they jerked awake the circle would be there,

just as round as if it had been drawn with a
compass.

Mum could have stayed the night too. She
was working with a journalist friend who'd
brought a tent along. Mum talked to Dan and
me about it, then she decided not to stay. It
was just a feeling she had that it wasn't a good
idea.

Dan and I always listened to Mum when
she got feelings about things. Even I could
remember how she'd said to Dad, just before
he went on that last trip, 'Do be careful, love.
I've got a feeling about it … I wish you weren't
going.'

Dad had worked for INTERSTEL airways, on the crash investigation team. He was an instrument specialist. This time he hadn't been investigating a crash, but several pilots had reported interference with their instruments over the Mojave' Desert. They'd managed to correct the problems manually so far, but the airline was quietly panicking. Dad had been working on a computer model, trying to find some pattern in what was going on. I don't remember much about that time, but Dan told me later that Dad had been up most of the night the week before he left. He was really worried. All he said to Dan and Mum was that a pattern kept coming up, and he didn't like the look of it.

Mum's feeling was right. Dad's plane crashed not far from Coyote Lake. Something went wrong with the instruments, they said: there'd been massive distortions caused by what looked like a powerful electrical storm. At least, that's what it looked like on the computer trace. But no storm showed up for hundreds of miles on the weather charts.

I asked Mum if she thought the corn circles really were made by aliens, like people said. She frowned, then she said, 'I don't know, Tony. I don't believe that the circles are made by UFOs landing. That would be much too obvious. The feeling I have is that we're being teased. Or tricked. As if someone – or something – is trying to distract us from what they're really doing.'

'What do you mean?'

'It's hard to explain, but try to put yourself in their place. If there really are aliens trying to get a foothold on our planet, I think they'd do it in a way we'd hardly even notice. There'd be changes, but not huge ones. After all, there are millions of us on this planet, and only a few of them. They'd come in very gradually over the years. They wouldn't want to risk being noticed – not too soon.'

'We'd be bound to notice, though, wouldn't we?'

'Not necessarily. Think of burglars. Some break in through the front door with crowbars, but others come in pairs pretending to be insurance salesmen. It's not till long after they've gone that you realise one of them's nipped upstairs and taken all your valuables. If there *were* aliens they wouldn't want to seem different. They'd want to seem like us. Part of normal life.'

So Mum thought the corn circles were there to keep us busy. To stop us noticing what else was going on. I shivered.

Dan was fifteen and a half, and I was almost eleven. You wouldn't think we'd be friends as well as brothers, but we always had been. Dan told me things he'd never tell Mum. He knew I'd never grass on him. And if something made him sad he could tell me that too. He had a music centre for his fifteenth birthday, much better than the one downstairs in the sitting room. He'd lie on his bed and I'd lie on the floor and we'd listen to his music and he'd tell me about what was going on with his friends; not all of it, but some. Enough. Dan had a Saturday job, so he always had money. And he'd talk to me about Genevieve. He knew I liked her. He'd had girlfriends before, but Genevieve was different.

That was another clue I didn't pick up straightaway. It was about five o'clock and Dan and I were home from school, but Mum wasn't back yet. The phone rang and I answered it. It was Genevieve. She asked how I was, the way she always did. She even remembered that I'd had to take my budgie to the vet, and asked if he was OK now. Then she said, 'Is Dan there, Tony?'

'Yes, I'll just get him.'

I turned round. Dan was lounging in the doorway, watching me.

'It's Genevieve,' I said, holding out the phone, but Dan didn't take it. He just kept on looking at me. It's hard to describe what happened next. I hadn't really been thinking about what was going on, because I was just doing something I'd done loads of times before, taking a call for Dan and passing it on to him. And since it was Genevieve I knew he'd be pleased.

But he wasn't pleased this time. He didn't react at all. I felt as if I was searching Dan's face for someone who wasn't there, like you'd search an empty house for a light in the windows.

'It's *Genevieve*!' I hissed, thinking perhaps he hadn't heard, and wishing I'd pressed the silence button in case Genevieve had. But Dan just shook his head, very slightly, as if he was making fun of me. Or Genevieve. And I was left holding the phone.

'I'm sorry, Genevieve,' I gabbled. 'He just went out, I think. I mean, I thought he was here, but he isn't.'

It must have sounded like a lie, but Genevieve isn't a suspicious sort of person.

'Oh, that's OK, Tony,' she said. 'I'll try again later. See you,' and she put the phone down. Her voice was just the same as always. You know how some people's voices make you feel that good things are about to happen? Genevieve had that sort of voice.

Dan's voice was cold and irritated. I couldn't believe I was hearing him right. 'I wish she'd stop bothering me,' he said.

'What?'

'You heard. I said I wish she'd stop bothering me. That girl really bugs me. If she calls again, say you don't know when I'll be back. No. Never mind. I'll take the phone.'

He held his hand out for it. Darkness looked out of his eyes, and blankness. There was no Dan there at all. He took the phone and held it up as if he was going to dial straightaway. The silver antenna poked out at the side of his head. I felt a shiver go through me. The antenna. Dan's dead eyes. Something scratched at the back of my mind, wanting to be let in:

'That's why they spend all their time on the phone, so they can keep in touch with all the other aliens ...'

I stared at Dan and he stared back at me. Mocking, as if he knew something I didn't.

And in a way ... almost frightening. And then I heard Mum's key go into the front door lock.

Dan stopped looking at me. By the time Mum called hello to us, he was already on his way up the stairs, calling back 'Homework' as he went. That was strange, too. Dan usually made Mum a cup of coffee when she got in from work. His bedroom door banged with the sort of bang that tells everyone else to keep out. I waited to hear the music; Dan always turned on his music as soon as he got into his room. But nothing happened. It was absolutely silent, as if there was no Dan in there at all.

That was the first evening Dan didn't eat supper. He'd been into Burger King with Alex on his way back from school. Mum didn't bother about it: she was tired and upset because she and her journalist friend had had an argument with their editor. The editor didn't like the idea of aliens coming in secretly while we were all busy with the corn circles. He wasn't going to run the feature unless they changed it.

The next day Dan said he had to finish a piece of coursework and could he take a sandwich and a glass of milk up to his room.

I don't remember all the excuses for not eating after that, at breakfast and tea and supper. They were never the same twice. Dan had always been clever, but now he was cunning too. He emptied his wastepaper basket every day now, so there was no chance of Mum finding the sandwiches he hadn't eaten. It was hard to know how much Mum had noticed. She never said anything, and she carried on giving Dan dinner money as usual.

It was three nights after the phone call from Genevieve that I couldn't sleep. My bedroom was next to Dan's, but I hadn't been into Dan's room for three days. Have you ever seen two magnets fighting one another with an invisible force field between them? There was one of those force fields at Dan's bedroom door. You couldn't see it, you couldn't touch it, but it was there. Even Mum found excuses not to go in there. She was collecting the dirty washing one afternoon when Dan was late home, and she said, 'I ought to have a sock-search under Dan's bed,' but she didn't go in. She hesitated by his door, then she said, 'No. He's old enough to sort out his own dirty washing,' and she walked past into my room to change my duvet cover.

I kept turning over and over in bed. I was used to falling asleep to the sound of Dan's music, and I couldn't settle down in the silence. What was he doing? Was he sitting there? Reading? Working? I knew there wasn't anyone else in his room, though usually Dan had his friends round a lot, and often they stayed late. None of his friends had been round for the past three days. And I don't know what he'd said to Genevieve, but she hadn't called again.

I tossed back the duvet and it flumped on to the floor. I found myself tiptoeing across the carpet, easing the door handle down, pulling the door open very gently. The landing light was on. Everything was quiet and Mum's door was shut too. 12:37 on my watch. She'd be asleep. My heart thudded as I crept close to Dan's door. Yes, it was still there, the invisible hand pushing me away, saying I wasn't wanted there. But I wasn't going to take any notice this time. This was Dan, my brother. I took a breath, and touched his door handle. Something fizzed on my fingers, like a tiny electric charge, like a rush of static electricity. I pulled my hand away and stepped back. Then I stopped myself.

'It's only Dan,' I told myself fiercely. 'It's only Dan.'

This time the prickle of electricity wasn't so bad, or perhaps it was because I was expecting it. Very gently I pushed the handle down. It didn't squeak or click. Then I pushed the door. As it opened a narrow strip of light fell from the landing into the darkness of Dan's room. It lit up Dan's bed, which was opposite the door. It lit up Dan, who was sitting up on the bed, fully dressed, reading. Reading in the dark. It lit up Dan's eyes as he turned to me, not at all surprised, as if he'd been expecting me. As if he'd seen me through the door.

'Hi,' he said, and turned a page.

There was only one switch for the main light, and it was by the door. It was off. I opened the door wider, so that more light came in, and walked across to Dan's bed. Casually, I touched his bedside light. It was cold. It hadn't been on at all. He'd really been reading in the dark – unless he'd been pretending? Unless he was trying to trick me and he'd been sitting there with the book, waiting for me to come in? But then how had he known I was going to come in?

There wasn't an answer. There was only Dan sitting on his bed. He didn't look as if he liked me much.

'I can't sleep,' I said. 'I'm going down to make some hot chocolate. Do you want some?'

'No,' said Dan. A week ago he'd have come down with me so I wouldn't make too much noise and wake up Mum. He'd have whipped up the chocolate, the way he does.
Suddenly I had an idea.

'I'm going to make a bacon sandwich,' I said, and waited for Dan to say what he always said: 'You make a bacon sandwich? Don't make me laugh. Let the man from the army do it.'
And then he'd make it for me.

He didn't. But something went over his face. Just for a second, there was a flicker of the real Dan, and as soon as I saw it I knew for sure that whoever else had been there the past three days, it hadn't been Dan. Then his face went back to the not-Dan face. The alien face. I felt the back of my neck prickle. Maybe it was the electricity, tingling around the room. Out of the corner of my eye I caught a movement. It was the minute hand of Dan's electric wall clock, racing crazily round and round in a perfect circle.

The thing inside my brother looked straight at me, daring me to say what I'd seen. The prickle ran up my arms and down. I'd run into a storm, just the way Dad had done, only here it wasn't as strong. There was only one of them here. I shook my head to clear the buzzing of my thoughts. Dan needed me.

'I really fancy a bacon sandwich,' I said again. 'We've got all the stuff. White bread, tomatoes, ketchup – and Mum bought some back bacon yesterday.'

Something struggled in his eyes again, like the ghost of my brother. It wasn't winning. Dan wanted so much to come back, but he couldn't. There was something else there, something alien, and it was too strong for Dan. It meant to stay, and it meant to keep Dan out of his own body. But at least now I felt I knew what I was fighting. What we were fighting. Dan hadn't eaten anything for three days. I knew he hadn't. He must be hungry. Whatever was in him now didn't need food, not our earth food. But Dan did. And Dan would do anything for a bacon sandwich. Perhaps, if I could take him by surprise somehow, and get him to eat – could that break whatever power this thing had over him? I didn't know, but it was worth trying.

'See you downstairs if you change your mind,' I said.

Our neighbours have a baby which cries in the night, so Mum goes to bed with cotton wool in her ears. Even so, I moved quietly as I lit the gas, got out the heavy frying pan, found bacon and tomatoes in the fridge, rummaged in the cupboard for ketchup. I just hoped the smell of frying bacon wouldn't wake her.

I put the frying pan on, melted a bit of fat, and lowered the bacon on the slice. It fizzled. After a minute the first tantalising wisp of the smell of frying bacon began to wreathe round the kitchen. Soon it would be through the door, then up the stairs, then under Dan's door. I turned up the heat carefully. I didn't want it to burn. The bacon spluttered, making a friendly sound in the kitchen. I laid the bread ready, and the sliced tomatoes, and the ketchup bottle. A drop of hot fat sparked on to the back of my hand and I sucked it away.

Dan. Dan. Dan.

'Dan'd go to Mars and back if he thought he'd get a bacon sandwich at the end of it,' Dad used to say. That was before Dad went.

The kitchen door opened. Dan walked slowly, as if he was pushing through something heavy. His face was pale, and it wasn't smooth and hard any more, the way it had been the past three days. It looked crumpled, as if he was trying to remember something.

'Your sandwich is nearly ready,' I said. I took the bacon off the heat, slid the slices out of the pan and laid them across the bread. I layered on the tomato and squeezed out just

 the right amount of ketchup. Then I cut the sandwich in half. Dan watched me all the time. I lifted my half, and took a bite. I saw him lick his lips, but he was shivering, as if he felt cold. And things were

moving behind his eyes, as if they were fighting for space there.

'Dan,' I said. 'Your sandwich is getting cold.'

His hands had dropped to his sides. They looked heavy. He didn't have the strength even to lift his hands, because all his strength was going into that fight inside him, between the Dan who was my brother and the stranger who wanted to make his home inside my brother's body. And that stranger was hanging on, tooth and claw. It wasn't going to let go easily.

I knew now for sure that it was nothing human that was looking at me out of Dan's eyes. It had come from far away, and all it cared about was its resting place. It was here for a purpose. It didn't care for Dan, or me or any of us. All it cared about was what it needed. Dan would never eat or sleep again if it had its way.

'Dan,' I said again. It felt as if his name was all I had. I came up close to him with his half of the sandwich still in my hand. He backed off a step or two, but then he didn't go any farther. I knew it was the real Dan who wanted to stay.

Suddenly I remembered something from far back, when I was sick with tonsillitis, not long after Dad died. It was when I was about six, I think. I had to take medicine four times a day, and I hated it. I used to press my lips tight shut and Mum couldn't make me swallow it. Then Dan took the spoon. He didn't seem worried, like Mum, and he didn't have any doubt that I'd open my mouth. He just put the spoon near my lips, without trying to push it into my mouth, and he said, 'Come on, babes. Do it for me.' And I did, every time, four times a day till I was better.

The words had been like magic to me then, when I was a little kid. Would they work now? Could they be the one thing that would bring Dan back and help him to fight off that powerful and lonely thing which had come to make its home in him?

I held the bacon sandwich up to Dan's mouth. His face was sweaty and he was breathing hard, as if he'd been running a long way.

'Come on, babes,' I whispered. 'Do it for me.'

I held my breath. I said it again, but silently.

Then, like something in slow motion, Dan's
mouth opened. I could see how hungry he was.
How much he wanted to come home. I felt the
electric prickle again, the one I'd felt when I
first tried to open Dan's door. It was stronger
now. It was trying to beat up a storm. It was
fighting me, as well as Dan. But this time it
wasn't going to win.

Dan bit down. He bit into the white bread, the bacon which was still hot, the juicy tomato. I saw the marks of his teeth in the bread. He chewed, and he swallowed the bacon sandwich. Then I looked at him and it was like looking at a house where all the lights have come on at once after it's been empty for a long time. His hands weren't heavy any more. He grasped the sandwich, bit again, and in a minute he'd finished it.

'You going to make me another, Tony, or have I got to show you how the man from the army makes a bacon sandwich?' he asked, and he smiled.

I didn't even jump when Mum opened the kitchen door. I knew it was her, not the thing which had been here and which was gone now, away through lonely space and places I couldn't begin to imagine, looking for somewhere else to make its home. Mum pulled the cotton wool out of her ears.

'You boys,' she said. 'I should have known. I was dreaming about bacon sandwiches.'

I don't know how Dan made it up with Genevieve, but the next day she was round at our house again. Dan's bedroom door was open, and his music was throbbing through the house. Mum didn't tell him to turn it down. She was in a wonderful mood because the editor had rung her back. He'd changed his mind and he was going to run the story about the corn circles in the way Mum and her friend wanted. For some reason he'd suddenly come to think it was worth printing the theory about aliens operating like bogus insurance salesmen, distracting us with corn circles and stealing our valuables when we weren't looking.

I asked Mum, 'Does the editor have kids?'

'Yes, he's got a teenage daughter. She's been a bit of a problem lately, apparently – he was telling me.' Mum glanced round, saw Dan was laughing with Genevieve, and whispered, 'His daughter's been acting a bit like Dan has these past few days, I think. But he says she's got over it, too.'

Genevieve stayed to supper, and you can guess what we ate. While we were eating it, I thought of what had happened the night before, in our midnight kitchen.

'Aliens don't eat bacon sandwiches,' I thought, looking at my brother.

Miss Mountain

Written by Philippa Pearce
Illustrated by Rosamund Fowler

Whatever else might be spring-cleaned in Grandmother's house, it was never her box-room. Old Mrs Robinson lived in a house with only two rooms upstairs, besides the bathroom: one was her bedroom; the other the box-room. This room fascinated her grandchildren, Daisy and Jim. It was about eight feet by six, and so full of stuff that even to open the door properly was difficult. If you forced it open enough to poke your head round, you saw a positive mountain of things reaching almost to the ceiling – old suitcases, bulging cardboard boxes of all shapes and sizes, stringed up parcels of magazines, cascades of old curtains, and a worm-eaten chair or two.

Grandmother was teased about the state of her boxroom. She retorted with spirit: 'There isn't as much stuff as there seems to be, because it's all piled up on the spare bed. The room's really a guest-room. I'm only waiting for a bit of time to clear it.'

Then everybody would laugh – Daisy and Jim and their father, who was Grandmother's son, and their mother, who was her daughter-in-law. Grandmother would join in the laughter. She always laughed a lot, even at herself.

If they went on to suggest lending a hand in the clearing of the box-room, Grandmother stopped laughing to say, 'I'd rather do it myself, thank you, when I have a bit of time.' But she never seemed to have the bit.

She was the nicest of grandmothers: rosy to look at, and plump, and somehow cosy. She liked to spoil her grandchildren. Daisy and Jim lived on an estate only just round the corner from Grandmother's little house, so they were always calling on her, and she on them.

Then suddenly everything was going to change.

The children's father got another job that would mean the whole family's moving out of the district, leaving Grandmother behind.

'Goodness me!' Grandmother said, cheerful about most things. 'It isn't the end of the world! I can come and visit you for the day.'

'Not just for the day,' said young Mrs Robinson, who was very fond of her mother-in-law. 'You must come and stay – often.'

'And the children shall come and stay with me,' Grandmother said.

'Where shall we sleep?' Jim asked.

'You'll have to clear the guest-room,' Daisy said.

'Yes, of course,' said her grandmother, but for a moment looked as if she had not quite foreseen that and regretted the whole idea.

But really the clearing out of the box-room ought to have been done years and years ago.

Grandmother said that she preferred to do all the work herself; but everyone insisted that it would be too much for her. In the end she agreed to let Daisy and Jim help her. Perhaps she thought they would be easier to manage than their parents.

How much the box-room held was amazing, and everything had to be brought out and sorted carefully. A lot went straight into the dustbin; some things – such as the bundles of magazines and the curtaining – went to the Church Hall for the next jumble sale; the chairs went onto the bonfire. Grandmother went through all the suitcases and got rid of everything; the suitcases themselves were only fit for jumble. The cardboard boxes, Grandmother said, were going to be more difficult; so for the moment they were piled up in a corner of her bedroom.

They sorted and cleared for several days. Sure enough under the mountain, there really had been a bed – narrow but quite wide enough for Daisy (who was older and larger than Jim), and there was a mattress on it, and pillows and blankets (only one moth-eaten enough for the dustbin). Grandmother made the bed up at once with sheets and pillowcases from her airing-cupboard.

'There!' she said. 'My guest-room!'

Daisy and Jim loved it. The room seemed so small and private, with an old-fashioned wallpaper that must have been there before Grandmother moved in, all those years ago. The window looked over the garden and received the morning sun. (Of course, that meant that in the evening the room dimmed early.)

All that remained was to clear the cardboard boxes still in Grandmother's own bedroom. She said she could do this herself in the evening when the children had gone home. But Daisy thought her grandmother already looked tired. She made her sit down in a chair and the two children began going through the boxes for her. 'We'll show you everything as we come to it,' Daisy said.

Grandmother sighed.

For the first half hour, everything went out to the dustbin – the cardboard boxes themselves and their contents, which turned out to be certificates of this and that and old programmes and views and other souvenirs. Then they came to boxes of photographs, some of them framed. These delayed the children.

'Look, Daisy!' said Jim. 'What a fat little girl!'

'Here she is again,' said Daisy. 'Just a bit

older and even fatter.'

'It's me,' said their grandmother, and leant forward from her chair to dart a hand between the two children and take the photographs and tear them in halves as rubbish.

'Grandmother!' they protested; but it was too late.

They found a framed wedding group of long ago with gentlemen in high-buttoning jackets and ladies wearing long dresses and hats toppling with feathers and flowers and fruit and bows.

'Was this your wedding, Grandmother?'

Grandmother said: 'I'm not as old as *that*. I wasn't thought of then. That was the wedding of my mother and father.'

The children peered. 'So that's our great-grandfather and our great-grandmother ...'

'And a couple of your great great aunts as bridesmaids,' said their grandmother. She snorted. 'I preferred not to go in for bridesmaids.' She found them a photograph of her own wedding, with everybody still looking very strange and old-fashioned, but clearly their grandmother did not think so.

The children thought that the quaint wedding group of their great grandparents would suit the little guest-room. With their grandmother's agreement, they hung it there. All the other photographs went down to the dustbin.

The last of the cardboard boxes was a squarish one, from which Daisy now drew out a barrel-shaped container. The staves of the barrel and the bands encircling them, and the lid, were all of the same tarnished metal.

Grandmother said, 'That's a biscuit barrel.'

'Is it real silver?' asked Daisy.

'Yes,' said Grandmother.

'How grand!' said Jim.

'Yes,' said Grandmother. 'Very valuable.'

Daisy set the biscuit barrel respectfully on the floor where they could all admire it.

'It was in our house when I was a child,' said Grandmother. 'I never liked it.'

'There's a curly H on it,' said Jim.

'For Hill,' said Grandmother. 'That was our surname. But I hated that biscuit barrel. I've always meant to get rid of it.'

'Please, Grandmother!' cried Daisy. 'You could stand it on the sideboard downstairs. It would look so nice. I'll polish up the silver.' Their grandmother still stared unforgivingly at the barrel. 'Think, Grandmother: you could keep biscuits in it for when we come to stay. Our favourite biscuits. I like custard-creams best.'

'I like pink sugar wafers,' said Jim.

'Promise you'll keep it, Grandmother, to keep our biscuits in,' said Daisy.

Grandmother stopped looking at the biscuit barrel and looked at her grandchildren instead. Suddenly she jumped up to hug them. 'Oh, yes!' she said. 'For, after all, I'm lucky. Very, very lucky. I've a guest-room and two grandchildren who want to come and stay with me!'

The little guest-room, so small and private, was ready for its first guest.

The first guest was Jim. Perhaps by rights it should have been Daisy, because she was the elder, but Jim was the one likely to be a nuisance during the family's house-removal. So the night before the removal and the first night after the removal were spent by Jim in his grandmother's guest-room. Then his father drove over and fetched him back to their new home.

In the new house, everyone was tired with the work of getting straight, and might have been short-tempered with Jim's little-boy bounciness. But Jim was quieter than usual. They asked whether he had had a good time with his grandmother. Yes, he had gone shopping with her, and she had bought him a multi-coloured pen; and he had had sparklers in the garden after dark; and peaches for both his suppers; and Grandmother had had pink sugar wafer biscuits for him – his favourite.

'You're lucky to have a grandmother like that,' said his mother.

'Reminds me of my own granny', said his father, 'your grandmother's mother. She was a good sort too.'

That night Daisy and Jim had to share a bedroom, because Daisy's room wasn't ready yet.

Jim went to bed, and asked his mother to leave the landing light on and the door ajar. 'I thought you'd given that up,' she said. 'You're a big boy now.' But she let him have his way.

Later, when Daisy came up, he was still awake. Daisy said, 'I'll be in my own room tomorrow night.'

'I don't mind sharing.'

Daisy got into bed.

'Daisy …'

'What?'

'I don't want to sleep here alone tomorrow night.'

'But – but, Jim, you always sleep alone!' There was no reply from the other bed. 'Jim, you're just being silly!'

Still no reply; and yet a little noise. Daisy listened carefully: Jim was crying. She got out of bed and went to him. 'What is it?'

'Nothing.'

'It must be something.'

'No, it's not. It's nothing.'

Daisy knew Jim. He could be very obstinate. Perhaps he would never tell her about whatever it was.

'You'd feel better if you told me, Jim.'

'No I shouldn't.'

He was crying so much that she put her

arms round him. It struck her that he was shivering.

'Are you cold, Jim?'

'No.'

'Then why are you shivering? You're not afraid of something?'

In answer, Jim gave a kind of gasp. 'Let me alone.'

Daisy was extremely irritated – and curious, too. 'Go on – say something. I shan't let you alone till you say something.'

Still he did not speak and Daisy amended, 'If you say something, I won't argue – I'll go back to bed and let you alone. But you must say something – something that *is* something.'

Jim collected himself; said carefully, 'I don't want to stay the night in Grandmother's house again – ever.' He turned over in bed with his back to Daisy.

Daisy stared at him, opened her mouth, remembered her promise, shut up, went back to bed and lay there to think.

She tried to think what might have happened during Jim's visit to make him feel as he did. It occurred to her that she might find out when her turn for a visit came …

How odd of Jim. There could be nothing to be afraid of at night in the house of the cosiest, rosiest, plumpest of grandmothers.

The moment she fell asleep, she was standing on her grandmother's front doorstep, her suitcase in her hand. She had already knocked. The door opened just as usual; there stood her grandmother, just as usual. But no, not as usual. Her grandmother peered at Daisy as if at a stranger. 'Yes?' she said.

'I'm Daisy Robinson,' said Daisy. 'I'm your granddaughter. I've come to stay the night.' Without a word, her grandmother stood aside to let her enter. At once Daisy began to mount the stairs that led to that early-shadowed little guest-room. She already saw the door ajar, waiting for her. Behind her, downstairs she could hear her grandmother securing the front door for the night – the lock, the bolts, the chain: she shut the two of them in together for the night. Daisy could hear her grandmother's little laugh: she was chuckling to herself.

The rest of the dream – if there were any had vanished by the time Daisy woke in the morning. All she knew of it was that she was glad she could not remember it.

Daisy told no one about Jim, chiefly because there was so little to tell. He seemed all right again, anyway. By that evening the bedrooms had been sorted out, so that Jim had his to himself. Without protest, he went to sleep alone. It's true that he screamed in the night, so that his mother had to go to him, but all children have nightmares sometimes. By the next night he had resumed his usual sound sleeping.

So Jim had been making a strange fuss about nothing: Daisy thought, or perhaps he'd got used to the idea of whatever there might have been, or – not the most comfortable idea for Daisy – he had been able to shut it from his mind because he was now a safe distance from Grandmother's little guest-room.

Their grandmother came to stay. She was
her usual cheerful self, and everyone enjoyed
the visit; Jim seemed to enjoy her company as
much as usual. At the end of her visit,
Grandmother said, 'Well, which of you two is
coming to sleep in my guest-room next?'

Jim said, 'It's Daisy's turn.'

'That's very fair of you, Jim,' their mother
said approvingly. Daisy looked at Jim but Jim
stubbornly looked past her. She knew that he
would not have agreed to go under any
circumstances.

Only a few weeks later, Daisy went.

With her suitcase, she stood on her
grandmother's doorstep. Twice she raised a
hand to the knocker and twice let it fall. The
third time, she really knocked. She heard the
patter of her grandmother's feet approaching.
The door opened, and there was Grandmother,
and all the uneasy feelings that Jim had given
her vanished away.

Her grandmother was laughing for joy at
her coming, and the house seemed to welcome
her. Even from the doorway Daisy could see
into the sitting-room, where the electric light
had not yet been switched on: an open fire
burned brightly, and by the fireplace stood a
tea-table with the china on it shining in the

firelight, and beyond that glowed the polish of the sideboard with the objects on it all giving as much glow or glitter as they could.

They had tea with boiled eggs and salad, as time was getting on and this had to be tea and supper together.

'Anything more you fancy, Daisy, dear?'

Daisy looked over to the sideboard, to the biscuit barrel. 'Pink sugar wafers?' she said.

'What an idea!' said her grandmother. 'They're not *your* favourite biscuits!'

Daisy went over to the biscuit barrel, put her hand in. 'Go on, dear, take whatever you find, as many as you want. I like you to do that.'

Daisy drew out a custard-cream biscuit. 'Grandmother, you're wonderful! You never forget anything.'

Grandmother sighed. 'Sometimes I wish I were more forgetful.'

Daisy laughed, and munched.

Later, they went to bed. They stood side by side looking into the little guest-room. With the curtains drawn and the bedside light glowing from inside a pink shade, the room looked as cosy and rosy as Grandmother herself. 'I hope you sleep well, my dear,' said her grandmother, and talked about the number of blankets and the number of pillows and the possibility of noise from neighbouring houses. Sometimes people had late parties.

'Did the neighbours disturb Jim?' Daisy asked suddenly.

'No,' said her grandmother. 'At least – he's a poor sleeper for such a young child, isn't he? He slept badly here.'

Daisy glanced sideways to see her grandmother's expression when she had said this. She found her grandmother stealing a sideways glance at her. They both looked away at once, pretending nothing had happened.

'Remember,' said Grandmother, 'if you want anything, I'm just across the landing.' She kissed Daisy good night.

Daisy decided not to think about that sideways glance tonight. She went to bed, slipped easily downhill into sleep, and slept.

Something woke her. She wasn't sure that it had been a noise but surely it must have been. She lay very still, her eyes open, her ears listening. Before going to bed she had drawn the curtains back so that she would wake to the morning sun: now it was night, without moon or stars, and all the lights of the surrounding houses had been extinguished.

She waited to hear a repetition of noise in the house; but there was none. She knew what she was expecting to hear: the creak of a stair-tread. There was nothing; but she became sure, all the same, that someone was creeping downstairs.

It could be – it *must* be – her grandmother going downstairs for something. She would go quietly, for fear of waking Daisy. But would she manage to go so very, very quietly?

Whoever it was would have reached the foot of the stairs by now. Still no noise.

It must be her grandmother; and yet Daisy felt that it wasn't her grandmother. And yet again she felt it was her grandmother.

She must know. She called, 'Grandmother!', pitching her voice rather high to reach the bottom of the stairs. The sound she made came out scream-like.

Almost at once she heard her grandmother's bedroom door open and the quick, soft sound of her feet bringing her across to the guest-room.

'Here I am, dear!'

'I thought I heard – I thought you were going downstairs, Grandmother.'

Grandmother seemed – well, agitated. 'Oh, did you? Sometimes I need a drink of water in the night and sometimes I do go downstairs for it.'

'But it wasn't you. You came from your bedroom just now, not back up the stairs.'

'What sharp ears you have, dear!'

'I didn't exactly *hear* anyone going downstairs, anyway,' Daisy said slowly.

'So it was all a mistake. That's all right then, isn't it?'

Not a mistake; more of a muddle, Daisy thought. But she let herself be kissed good night again, and her light was switched off. Her grandmother went back to bed. There was quiet in the house: not only no unusual sound, but no feel of anything unusual. Daisy slept until morning sunshine.

The daytime was made as delightful for Daisy as her grandmother had made it for Jim. But evening came, and night; and this night was far worse than the previous one.

Daisy woke and lay awake, knowing that someone was creeping downstairs again. But it's my imagination, she told herself; how can I know, when I hear nothing?

Whoever it was reached the bottom of the stairs and crossed the hall to the sitting-room door. Had Grandmother left that door shut or open when she went to bed? It did not matter. Whoever it was had entered the sitting room and was moving across to the sideboard.

What was happening down there in the dark and silence?

Suddenly there was no more silence. From downstairs there was a shrill scream, that turned into a crying and sobbing, both terrified and terrifying.

Hardly knowing what she was doing, Daisy was out of bed, through her bedroom door, across the landing to her grandmother's room. The door was shut: she had to pause an instant to open it, and in that instant she realised that the crying from downstairs had stopped.

She was inside her grandmother's bedroom. The bedside light was on and Grandmother, flustered, had just sat up in bed. Daisy said: 'That crying!'

'It was me,' said her grandmother.

'Oh, no, no, no, no!' Daisy contradicted her grandmother with fury. She glared at her in fury and terror – the nicest grandmother in the world was concealing something, lying. What kind of grandmother was she then: sly; perhaps treacherous? Wicked?

At the look on Daisy's face, Grandmother shrank back among the pillows. She hid her face in her hands. Between the fingers Daisy saw tears beginning to roll down over the dry old skin. Grandmother was crying, with gasping sobs, and her crying was not all that different, but much quieter, from the crying

Daisy had heard downstairs.

In the middle of her crying, Grandmother managed to say, 'Oh, Daisy!' and stretched out her hands towards her, begging her.

Daisy looked searchingly at her grandmother, and her grandmother met her gaze. Daisy took the outstretched hands and stroked them. She calmed herself even while she calmed her grandmother. 'I'll make us a pot of tea,' she said. 'I'll bring it up here.'

'No,' said her grandmother. 'I'll come down. We'll have it downstairs, and I'll tell you – I'll tell you –' She began to cry again.

Daisy was no longer afraid. She went downstairs into the kitchen to boil a kettle. As she went, she turned the sitting room light on, and switched on an electric fire. Everything was exactly as usual. The door had been shut.

From downstairs she heard her grandmother getting up and then coming out of her bedroom. She did not come directly downstairs: Daisy heard her cross the landing into the guest-room, spend a few moments there, then come down.

Daisy carried the tea on a tray into the sitting-room; she took the biscuit barrel off the sideboard and put it on the tray, in case Grandmother wanted something to eat with her tea. Grandmother was already waiting for her. She had brought downstairs with her the framed wedding photograph from Daisy's bedroom, and set it where they could both see it. Daisy asked no questions.

They sat together and sipped their tea. Daisy also nibbled a biscuit; her grandmother had shaken her head and shuddered when Daisy offered her the biscuit barrel.

'Now I'll tell you,' said Grandmother. She paused while she steadied herself, visibly. 'I brought the wedding photo down so that I could *show* you.'

Again she paused, for much longer, so Daisy said, 'Your mother looked sweet as a bride.'

'I never knew her,' said Grandmother. 'She died when I was very young.'

Daisy said, 'But Dad knew her! He talks about his granny.'

'That was my stepmother; his step-grandmother.'

Now something seemed plain to Daisy. 'A stepmother – poor Grandmother!'

'No,' said Grandmother. 'It wasn't like that at all. My stepmother – only I never really think of her as my stepmother, just as my mother – she was a darling.'

'Then –?'

'They're both in the group,' said Grandmother. 'My mother as the bride. My stepmother – as she later became – as one of the bridesmaids. The bridesmaids were my two aunts: one my mother's sister, whom my father married after my mother's death; the other my father's sister.'

Daisy studied the photograph. Now that she knew that one of the bridesmaids was the bride's sister, it was easy to see which – there was the same plumpness with prettiness.

The other bridesmaid was tall, thin and rather glum-looking. There was a resemblance between her and the bridegroom, but not such a striking one.

'When my mother died,' said Grandmother, 'I was a very little girl, still babyish in my ways, no doubt. My father had to get someone to look after me and to run the house. He was in business and away at his office all day. He asked his sister to come – the other bridesmaid.'

Daisy looked at the thin bridesmaid, and wondered.

'She'd always been very fond of my father, I believe, and jealous of his having married. Perhaps she was glad that my mother had died; perhaps she would have been glad if I had never been born. She would have had my father all to herself then. She hated me.'

'Grandmother!'

'Oh, yes, she hated me. I didn't fully understand it then. I just thought I had suddenly become stupid and disobedient and dirty and everything that – as it seemed to me – anyone would hate. I daresay I was rather a nasty little girl: I became so. One of the worst things was –'

Grandmother stopped speaking, shaded her face with her hand.

'Go on.'

'It won't seem terrible to you. You may just laugh. Aunt used to sneer. When she sneered, that made it worse.'

'But what was it?'

'I ate.'

'Well, but …'

'I ate whenever I could. I ate enormously at meals and I ate between meals. Aunt used to point it out to my father, and put a tape measure round where she said my waist should be, as I sat at table. I've always been plump, like my mother's side of the family: I grew fat – terribly fat.

'Our surname was Hill. There were two Miss Hills in the house, my aunt and myself. But Aunt said there need be no confusion – she was Miss Hill; I was Miss Mountain. She called me Miss Mountain, unless my father were present. She would leave notes to me, addressed to Miss Mountain. Once my father found one and asked her about it, and she pretended it was just a little joke between us. But it wasn't a joke – or if it were, it was a cruel, cruel one.'

'Couldn't you just have eaten less and grown thinner and spoilt her game?' asked Daisy.

'You don't understand. Her teasing of me made me eat even more. I took to stealing food. I'd slip out to the larder after Sunday dinner and tear the crisp bits of fat off the joint while it was still warm. Or I'd take sultanas out of the jar in the store-cupboard. Or I'd pare off bits of cheese. Even a slice of dry bread, if there were nothing else. Once I ate dog-biscuits from the shelf above the kennel.

'Of course, sooner or later, Aunt realised what was happening. She began to expect it and took a delight in catching me out. If she couldn't catch me at it she would prevent me.

She took to locking the kitchen door at night, because she knew I went down then to the store-cupboard and larder. Then I found the biscuit barrel.'

'This very biscuit barrel?'

'Yes. It always stood on the sideboard with cream crackers in it – just the plainest of biscuits, to be eaten with cheese. Well, I didn't mind that. I used to creep down for a cream cracker or two in the middle of the night.'

'In this house?'

'Goodness, no! We lived a hundred miles from here and the house has been pulled down now, I believe.

'Anyway, I used to creep down, as I've said. I daren't put on any light, although I was terribly afraid of the dark – I had become afraid of so many things by then. I felt my way into the room and across to the sideboard, and along it. The sideboard was rather grand, with a mirror, and all kinds of grand utensils were kept on it: the silver cream jug, a pair of silver candlesticks, the silver-rimmed bread board with the silver-handled bread-knife. I felt among them until I found the biscuit barrel. Then I took off the lid and put my hand in.'

She paused.

'Go on, Grandmother.'

'I did that trip once, twice, perhaps three times. The third or fourth time seemed just as usual. As usual I was shaking with fright, both at the crime I was committing and at the blackness in which I had to commit it. I had felt my way to the biscuit barrel. I lifted the lid with my left hand, as usual. Very carefully, as usual, I slipped my right hand into the barrel. I had thought there would be crackers to the top; but there were not. I had to reach towards the bottom – down – down – down – and then my fingers touched something and at once there was something – oh, it seemed like an explosion! – something snapped at me, caught my fingers, held them in a bitter grip, causing me pain, but far more than pain: terror. I screamed and screamed and sobbed and cried.

'Footsteps came hurrying down the stairs, lights appeared, people were rushing into the dining-room, where I was. My father, my aunt, the maidservant – they all stood looking at me, a fat little girl in her nightdress, screaming, with her right hand extended and a mouse-trap dangling from the fingers.

'My father and the servant were bewildered but I could see that my aunt was not taken by surprise. She had been expecting this, waiting for it. Now she burst into loud laughter.

'I couldn't bear it. With
my left hand I caught up the
silver-handled bread-knife from the sideboard
and I went for her.'

'You killed her?'

'No, of course not. I was in such a muddle
with screaming and crying, and the knife was
in my left hand, and my aunt side-stepped, and
my father rushed in and took hold of me and
took the knife from me. Then he prised the
mouse-trap off my other hand.

'All this time I never stopped crying. I think I was deliberately crying myself ill. Through my crying I heard my father and my aunt talking, and I heard my father asking my aunt how there came to be a mouse-trap inside the biscuit barrel.

'The next day either I was ill or I pretended to be – there wasn't much difference, anyway. I stayed all day in bed with the curtains drawn. The maid brought me bread and milk to eat. My aunt did not come to see me. My father came, in the morning before he went to his office, and in the evening when he got home. On both occasions I pretended to be asleep.

'The day after that I got up. The fingers of my right hand were still red where the trap had snapped across them, and I rubbed them to make them even redder. I didn't want to be well. I showed them to the maidservant. Not only were the fingers red but two of the finger-nails had gone quite black. The maid called my father in – he was just on his way to work.

'He said that the doctor should see them and the maid could take me there that afternoon on foot. Exercise would do me good, and change. He looked at me as if he were about to say more but he did not. He did not mention my aunt – who would have been the person to take me to see the doctor, ordinarily – and there was still no sign of her.

'The maid took me. The doctor said my fingers had been badly bruised by the blow of the mouse-trap but nothing worse. The fingernails would grow right. I was disappointed. I had hoped that my finger bones were broken, that my fingertips would drop off. I wanted to be sent into hospital. I didn't want to go home and be well and go on as before: little Miss Mountain as before.

'I walked home with the maid. As we neared our house, I saw a woman turn in at our gateway. When we reached the gate, she was walking up the long path to the front door.

'Now I've said I never knew my own mother, to remember; but when I saw the back view of that young woman – she *stumped* along a little, as stoutish people often do – I knew that that was exactly what my mother had looked like. I didn't think beyond that; that was enough for me. I ran after her, as fast as I could; and, as she reached the front door, I ran into her. She lost her balance, she gave a cry between alarm and laughter, and sat down suddenly on the front doorstep, and I tumbled on top of her and felt her arms round me, and burrowed into her, among the folds of all the clothing that women wore in those days.

'I always remember the plump softness and warmth of her body, and how sweet it was. I cried and cried for joy, and she hugged me.

'That was my other aunt, the other bridesmaid – my mother's sister. My father had telegraphed for her to come from the other side of England, and she had come. My father had already sent my thin aunt packing – I never saw her again.

'My plump aunt moved in as housekeeper, and our house was filled with laughter and happiness and love. Within the year, my father had married her. She had no child of her own by him, so I was her only child. She loved me, and I her.'

'Did you – did you manage to become less stout?' Daisy asked delicately.

'I suppose I must have done. Anyway, I stopped stealing food. And the biscuit barrel disappeared off the sideboard – my new mother put it away, after she'd heard the story, I suppose. Out of sight, out of mind: I forgot it. Or at least I pretended to myself that I'd forgotten it. But whenever it turns up, I remember. I remember too well.'

'I've heard of haunted houses,' said Daisy thoughtfully. 'But never of a haunted biscuit barrel. I don't think it would be haunted if you weren't there to remember, you know.'

'I daresay.'

'Will you get rid of it, Grandmother? Otherwise Jim will never come to stay again; and I – I –'

'You don't think I haven't wanted to get rid of it, child?' cried her grandmother. 'Your grandfather wouldn't let me; your father wouldn't let me. But no – that was never the real explanation. Then, I couldn't bring myself to give them my reasons – to tell the whole story; and so the memory has held me like a trap. Now I've told the story; now I'm free; now the biscuit barrel can go.'

'Will you sell it, Grandmother? It must be worth a lot of money.'

'No doubt.'

'I wonder how much money you'll get and what you'll spend it on, Grandmother …'

Grandmother did not answer.

The next morning Daisy woke to sunshine and the sound of her grandmother already up and about downstairs. Daisy dressed quickly and went down. The front door was wide open and her grandmother stood outside on the doorstep, looking at something further up the street. There was the sound of a heavy vehicle droning its way slowly along the street, going away.

Daisy joined her grandmother on the doorstep and looked where she was looking. The weekly dustbin van was droning its way along: it had almost reached the end of the street. The men were slinging into it the last of the rubbish that the householders had put out for them overnight or early this morning. The two rows of great metal teeth at the back of the van opened and closed slowly, mercilessly on whatever had been thrown into that huge maw.

Grandmother said, 'There it goes,' and at once Daisy knew what 'it' was. 'Done up in a plastic bag with my empty bottles and tins and the old fish-finger carton and broken eggshells, and I don't know what rubbish else. Bad company – serve it right.' The van began to turn the corner. 'I've hated it,' said Grandmother. 'And now it's being scrunched to pieces. Smashed to smithereens.' Fiercely she spoke; and Daisy remembered the little girl who had snatched up a bread-knife in anger.

The van had turned the corner.

Gone.

Grandmother put her arm round Daisy and laughed. She said: 'Daisy, dear, always remember that one can keep custard-creams and pink sugar wafers for friends in any old tin.'

The Airman's Sixpence

Written by Helen Dunmore

Illustrated by David Frankland

She keeps me up with her every night. It's as if she doesn't want to be alone. Even though it's nearly eleven o'clock now, she's just put three more big logs onto the fire. My cocoa steams on the wonky tin tray. She keeps back enough milk for my cocoa every night, and even sugar. Two spoonfuls. She always saves her sugar ration for me. There are biscuits as well. She watches me eating and her face is hungry. It's no good trying to hide a biscuit for Billy. She sees every move I make.

'Drink up, dear. Don't you like your cocoa?'

'Mmm, yeah. Course I do,' and I pick up the thick white mug.

'There's no need to say "yeah", Ruby. After all, we aren't Americans.'

'No, Mrs Penbury.'

'Auntie Pauline, dear! You silly girl.' And she laughs, a tinkly laugh that's a bit frightening because it doesn't seem to belong to her. Mrs Penbury is big, and she's as strong as any man. She does a man's job. She's always telling us that. Men have to be hard.

The wind whines round the farmhouse. It sounds as if it's fingering the walls, trying to get in to us. But I don't mind the wind.

I strain my ears for what I think I can hear under it. Yes, there it is. A sound that's even thinner, even sadder than the wind. I glance quickly at her, and clatter my mug down on the tray to cover the sound. Has she heard? She's frowning, staring at her feet. What if she gets up, goes to the stairs, listens? What if she hears him? I'm sure it's Billy. He'll have had another of his bad dreams.

Billy's five. He never used to have bad dreams, till we came here.

We were in London before, with Mum, then before that we were down in Devon, with Mrs Sands. She was lovely. But she couldn't take us back when the bombing started again, because her daughter, Elsie, had a new baby. Mum didn't want to send us away again, but she got a job in the factory at nights, and that meant she couldn't take us to the air-raid shelter if a raid started. I would've taken Billy. I'm old enough. But Mum wouldn't let me.

'No, Rube. With you and Billy safe in the country, at least I've got peace of mind. I know I'm doing right by you.'

It was all right in Devon with Mrs Sands. We missed Mum, of course we did. But not like this. Not with a pain that gets worse every morning when I wake up and know we've got another day here.

It *is* Billy. I know it is. He's crying again. He isn't properly awake yet, or he wouldn't make a sound. He's crying in his sleep. I shuffle my feet, crunch my biscuit, slurp the rest of my cocoa.

'I'm ever so tired, Auntie Pauline. I think I'd better get to bed.'

She stares at me. 'I've only just put those logs on the fire,' she says. 'Don't you want to sit up a bit longer?'

She always wants me to sit up. I don't think she wants to be on her own. She likes me to keep talking, it doesn't matter what I say. When it's quiet, she looks as if she's listening out for things I can't hear.

But I've got to get to Billy. I stand up, and put down my mug. I'm supposed to kiss her goodnight now. I've got to do it. She mustn't know that I don't like kissing her, or she'll be worse than ever to Billy. Her hair bristles against my face.

'G'night, Auntie Pauline.'

'Goodnight, Ruby. There's a good girl.'

There's a little oil lamp for me to carry up and undress by. Billy has to go up in the dark. She pretends it's because he's too young to remember about the blackout, and he might show a light. Billy is frightened of the dark.

I go up the creaky stairs with my lamp flame shivering and bobbing on the walls. They are rough, uneven walls because this is an old house, right on the edge of the village and well away from the other houses. It's a lonely house. Maybe that's why she wants me to sit up with her, even though at home Mum would've sent me to bed ages ago.

The whimpering sound is getting louder. I hurry. She mustn't hear it. I know what to do.

I've got to wake him up really gently. I kneel
down by his bed and put my arms softly round
him. He's sitting up but I can tell he's still
asleep. His eyes have that funny nightmare
look in them. He is cold. I cuddle him close
and whisper, 'Billy, it's all right. It's only me.
It's Ruby.'

I keep on cuddling and whispering. Slowly
his stiff body relaxes. I can feel him coming out
of the dream and waking up. I press his face
into my shoulders to hide the noise.

'It's OK, Billy, Ruby's here.'

He's shaking. Perhaps he's ill? But I look at
his face by the oil lamp and I see he's crying.

Fear pounces on me.

'Oh, Billy. You haven't. You haven't gone and done it again.'

And he nods his head, crying and shivering.

'Never mind. Don't cry. Ruby's here.' I hold him tight, tight. He's only five. My little brother, Billy.

'You look after Billy, Rube. You know how he gets his asthma.'

That's what Mum said when she was waving us off on the train, the second time we were evacuated. She thought it would be like Mrs Sands' again, and so did we. Billy was all excited, jumping up to look out of the window, waving at Mum. *'You look after Billy.'*

Yes, I was right. He's wet himself. It's not his fault. It happens when he's asleep. He can't help it. But she mustn't find out. What can I do?

I can't do anything. She'll find out. She always does. And she'll put Billy in the cupboard under the stairs again, for hours and hours. It's dark in there. She says it's to teach him. *'He can't go on like this, Ruby. What'll your mum say when she gets him back, wetting the bed every night? She'll think I don't know what's right. Sometimes you've got to be cruel to be kind.'*

He doesn't cry or scream when he's in the cupboard. I think she thinks he doesn't care. Oh, Billy. *'He's a boy, Ruby. No good bringing him up soft. You won't be doing him any favours.'*

Suddenly I make up my mind.

'Stand still, Billy, while I get your clothes. We're going home.'

I scrabble through the drawers. Clean pants, clean trousers, Billy's warmest jersey. His winter coat is on the hook downstairs. I'll get him dressed then we'll both get into bed and wait, wait … Once she's gone to bed, we'll go. We'll go home. Mum wouldn't want us to stay here. I know she wouldn't. She'll be working now, she works nights in the factory, but by the time we get to London it'll be morning. I don't care about the bombs.

When the last sound of Auntie Pauline going to bed has died away, we wait to give her time to go to sleep. I've blown out the lamp and it's dark. But I know my way round the house, even in the dark. I know all its lonely corners.

'Billy. Ssh. Hold my hand.'

The stairs don't creak. The kitchen door opens and there's the smell of the slack she's put on the fire to bank it up for the night.

Billy presses up behind me while I slide the big bolt back, very very slowly. It squeaks like a mouse. She hates mice. She's always leaving poison for them. The yard door swings open and black cold night air fills the space in the door frame.

'Wait there, Billy. Don't move.'

I sweep my hand along the dresser. There it is. Her fat black purse with the big clasp. I weigh the heavy purse in my hand. My mum always said she could leave a penny out on the kitchen table all week.

'Ruby'd never touch it. Would you, Rube?'

'No, Mum!'

I was so proud of that. Mum let me go to her purse and get the shopping money out, because she knew I'd never take a penny off her. Now I unsnap Auntie Pauline's big purse and feel inside. Two heavy half-crowns. A couple of joeys. A sixpence and a florin. I take them all and wrap my handkerchief round them. Is it enough to get us to London?

I hold Billy's hand tight as we shut the kitchen door behind us. The yard is full of shadows and we dodge through them to the gate. The lane is a tunnel of night.

'We can't go through the village,' I whisper

to Billy. 'All the dogs'll bark at us. We'll go down the lane and across the fields.'

My chest hurts. Billy's too little, he can't run like I can. I hoist him up and carry him but he's too heavy for me and I can't carry him for long. He runs a bit, then I carry him, then he runs again. Each time I pick him up, he's heavier.

'You're a good runner, Billy!' I tell him, to keep him going.

The wind rustles the trees over our heads. There are sudden shapes and shadows. Something barks. Maybe a fox. We know about country things now.

Then we come round the corner of the lane and a bit of moon shines on a big puddle. The road forks three ways.

'I got to put you down, Billy.'

He flops up against me. It's his asthma. Mum never ever lets him go out at night.

'All right, Billy, we'll have a rest.'

There's a stile and a path going across the fields. But no signposts. They've taken them all down in case the Germans come. Just the three lanes pointing off into the dark, and the path across the fields. Nowhere to say where the railway station is.

'You better now, Billy?'

He looks up and nods. I know he isn't, really. I stare round, trying to guess, trying to remember which direction the station is. We came from the station, off the London train. But it all looks different in the dark, strange and different.

'You wait here a minute while I look down the lane.'

But he grips me tight. 'Don't leave me, Rube!'

That's when I see it. A little red light that grows strong in the dark under the trees, then fades. Then it brightens again. I know at once what it is. My mum smokes and sometimes she comes in and sits on my bed in the dark and I watch the red tip of her cigarette winking at me. Someone's smoking, there under the trees. Someone I can't see. I grab hold of Billy. As we stare, a big shadow peels away from the trees and moves into the lane. It's a man. A man smoking. A man in uniform.

I know all the uniforms. I peer through the dark and I see the shape of him. RAF.

Straight away I feel a bit better. I like the RAF. He'll be on his way back to camp. Probably been to a dance. He throws away the cigarette and it skitters down the air and dies on the wet road. Then he walks slowly towards us as if he's been waiting for us, as if he knew we were going to come.

'Hello.'

I don't answer. But Billy pipes back, 'Hello' to him.

'You're out late,' says the airman. He's got a village voice, not a London voice like us. He must be from round here. I wonder where?

'Yeah,' I say. I look at him hard. Is it OK to ask him? I can see him quite well now because the clouds have blown back from the moon. But there's the shadow of his cap, too, hiding him.

I clench my hand in my pocket, and it knocks against the money I've stolen. She'll be after me. She'll get me. They'll all believe her. *A thief. A little thief.* No one'll believe I had to do it because of Billy, except Mum. I've got to get to Mum.

'We've got to catch a train,' I say. 'My mum's ill.'

'Oh,' he says. 'The London train? The milk train?'

'Yeah. The milk train.'

Then I think, *How did he know it was London I wanted*? But I don't ask.

'It's this way,' he says, pointing across the fields. 'It's only a mile, across the fields.' Then he says, 'I'll go with you. Make sure you get there safe.'

Everything my mum's told me about strangers floods into my head.

'It's all right,' I say quickly. 'We can find it.'

'Over this field. Turn left at the stile and follow the hedge. Then there's a gate. Straight over and across that field and you come to the road. Turn right and it takes you all the way.'

'Is there a bull?' asks Billy in his growly voice. He thinks every field's got a bull in it.

'Couple of cows if you're lucky. Turn left, keep going, cross the gate, keep going, turn right at the road. You got that?'

'Yeah.'

'Mind you look after Billy.'

Did he say that or was it my mum's voice in my head? No, he did. *How did he know Billy's name*?

'You got money for the train?'

My hand closes over *her* hard, cold coins.

'I got money.'

He looks at me. 'You took it, didn't you?

You don't want to go taking her money.' He digs his hand in his pocket and brings out a handful of notes and coins. He picks out two pound notes and a ten-shilling note and holds them out to me. But I step back.

'It's all right,' he says, 'You take it. I've no use for it now.'

So I do. I feel as if I've got to do what he says. Then he gives Billy a sixpence. 'Buy some sweets with it,' he says. Billy looks down at the sixpence and up at the airman. He doesn't smile or say thank you. Billy's always quiet when he's pleased.

The man puts his hand on Billy's head, and rumples his hair as if he knows him.

'Give me that money of hers,' he says to me. 'I'll put it back for you. Then you're all straight.'

I like the way he says it, as if he knows how I'm always all straight at home, with Mum. I'm not really a thief. I give him the handkerchief, and he unknots it and takes out the money. He puts it away carefully, in a separate pocket from his own money, then he looks at us again. This time the moon is full on his face. He is sort of smiling, but not quite, and under it he looks sad. He reminds me of someone. He looks like someone.

'Don't hold it against her,' he says. 'She can't help herself.'

I say nothing. He sounds as if he knows Auntie Pauline better than I ever could.

'Go on, then,' he says. I climb the stile, then he swings Billy up and over. I take Billy's hands and jump him down. 'I'll stand here,' says the airman, 'just to make sure you take the right turning.'

When we get to the other side of the field we look back and he's still there. He waves, pointing left, and I wave back to show I know what he means.

Then we climb up the next stile, and over, and the hedge hides him. We go as fast as we can. There's no time to talk, but once we're safely on the road, Billy pants out in his growly whisper, 'He's still watching us.'

'How d'you know?'

'He just is.'

The wind blows round us, cold and sweet and smelling of cows and country things. We stop to catch our breath and listen. Ahead of us there's the shunting noise of a train and I know we're nearly there.

'Don't worry, you're not going back,' says Mum. She's been working all night. She's worn out, and here we are on the doorstep and what's she going to do with us? But it doesn't matter. Nothing matters now we're home. Billy's thinner and his chest sounds worse, and when I tell Mum about the cupboard under the stairs she says she's going straight down the Evacuation Office to sort it out this very minute and we're not to move till she gets back. She goes off without even changing out of her overalls.

It's a long time before Mum comes back. Billy's asleep and I think I've been asleep, too. Things are all muddled up in my head. The airman, the dark lane, the feel of Auntie Pauline's money. How could he put it back? Mum flops into her chair and shuts her eyes.

'They're going to get on to her,' she says at last. 'Course, there's always another side to the story. Did she ever talk to you about her son, Ruby?'

'I didn't know she had a son. She didn't like boys.'

'He was in the Air Force. Died on a bombing raid last year. That's why she took you kids in, for the company. It must have been hard for her. Sent her a bit peculiar, I dare say, all on her own out there in the middle of nowhere, grieving for him. Not that it's any excuse, mind.'

'Don't be too hard on her. She can't help herself. Give me the money, I'll put it back.'

Mum sighs. 'I could murder a cup of tea,' she says.

'I'll make it,' I say quickly. I want something to do.

'Good girl. Seems she was so proud of him, being in the RAF. Oh, this war's got a lot to answer for. I suppose it got to her, other people's kids being all right when hers had gone.'

'But she was all right to me.'

'You're a girl, Rube. You wouldn't've reminded her of her son.'

I remember when Auntie Pauline was always saying, *'No good bringing a boy up soft. You're not doing him any favours.'*

Was she thinking of her boy, and the war that was waiting for him when he grew up? I put the match to the gas and wait for the kettle to boil. I listen to the water begin to hiss in the bottom of the kettle. It's a sleepy, peaceful sound, and I shut my eyes.

Moonlight shines on the airman's face. He looks like someone I know. Who is it? The answer itches at the back of my mind but I can't quite reach it. He smiles. Then I know. It's Billy. The airman looks like Billy. So that was it. Mum was right, it was because Billy reminded Auntie Pauline of her own son that she was so hard on him. But perhaps she didn't mean to be … perhaps she thought she was doing the right thing …

The kettle changes its note and starts to sing. I open my eyes and look at Billy, sleeping on the kitchen settle. His face has a bit of colour in it again. His hand is shut tight, even though he's asleep, and in it there's the airman's sixpence.